# Daily Readings from Prayers & Praises in the Celtic Tradition

# Daily Readings from Prayers & Praises in the Celtic Tradition

Introduced and edited by
## A. M. Allchin and Esther de Waal
*Illustrations from 'Carmina Gadelica'
and George Bain's 'Celtic Art'*

Templegate Publishers
Springfield, Illinois

First published in 1986 by
Darton, Longman and Todd Ltd
89 Lillie Road, London SW6 1UD


Introduction and arrangement © 1986
A. M. Allchin and Esther de Waal

ISBN 0-87243-151-7


First published in the United States in 1987 by
Templegate Publishers
302 E. Adams St./P.O. Box 5152
Springfield, Illinois 62705

## The Editors

A. M. Allchin is a Canon Residentiary of Canter-
bury Cathedral and the author of *The World is a
Wedding* (Crossroad), *The Kingdom of Love and
Knowledge* (Harper), and *The Joy of all Creation*
(Farrar, Straus & Giroux).

Esther de Waal is a historian and the author of
*Seeking God, the Way of St Benedict* (Liturgical
Press, Collegeville, Minn.), and *God Under my
Roof, Celtic Songs and Blessings* (Paraclete
Press, Orleans, Mass.).

# *Contents*

# Introduction

Putting together this anthology has been for both
editors an act of gratitude for all that the discovery
of the Celtic tradition has brought us. We hope
that others may find in its riches a vision which
deepens consciousness and extends horizons. For
one of us, growing up in London, the discovery
first of Wales and then of Ireland and Scotland
was like opening a door into a hitherto unsus-
pected part of the house in which you live.
Suddenly you find something that has always been
there. The island of Britain is larger than England.
Our familiar history – the kings and queens of
England – is part of a larger, more complex story.
And this discovery has an inner dimension to it.
The Celtic tradition is full of spiritual insight; it
touches hidden springs within us, 'the part of
myself that is older than I am'. For the other, the
possibilities of this exploration had been sensed
from childhood. Born into a Scottish family and
brought up in the Welsh border country, she had
the immeasurable advantage of a childhood and
youth spent on the edges of the mainstream. Later
on, coming to read more widely in other Celtic
sources, this rooting in a border country
continued to feed and colour her understanding.
For borderlands are ambiguous places, places in
which different cultures and histories meet, where
the familiar and the strange mix and challenge one
another. They can be mysterious and uncomfort-

able: they can be a frontier from which the new is opened up.

This is very much the way in which the collection which follows speaks to us. Throughout it there is much that is totally familiar, completely mundane, the daily and the ordinary. It would be difficult to be more thoroughly down to earth than a mother in the Outer Hebrides. And yet this can become the frontier to another world. The mundane is the edge of glory. Earth and heaven touch, interpenetrate, illuminate one another. The immediacy of the presence of God is here made urgent, accessible in all the unglamorous familiarity of daily life. And yet simultaneously we become aware of a sky white with angels' wings, throngs of saints, a glimpse of mystery.

We are grateful for a tradition which rejoices in creation and we owe much to the seeing eye of the eighth-century Irish hermit, whose sight, washed clean by contemplation, views the world with extraordinary clarity. But we are even more grateful for a tradition which will not let us enjoy a theology of creation without also presenting us with a theology of redemption and reminding us of the cross. We cannot have the light without the darkness. For, ultimately, we do not even want to evade the cost of discipleship by being allowed to escape into some sort of easygoing religion which glosses over the reality of sin and the need for repentance.

But to discover a tradition just because we need it can be a dangerous undertaking. It is vital to be strictly honest here and not to lapse into any sentimentality or romanticism which will merely find in the Celtic world material to feed contemporary needs and longings, and thus to remake the past in our own image. What follows should be allowed to speak for itself, with all its strangeness and complexity.

The passages we have chosen for this book reflect a great variety of places and periods. They come from the hidden, neglected side of the history of Britain and Ireland, from the peoples and languages of Ireland, Scotland and Wales. Some have the simplicity of a Christmas carol, one or two the sophistication of a poem composed by a professional poet for a princely household. Many come from people outwardly very poor and inconspicuous. They come from men and women of prayer with no more worldly status or qualification than the apostles. Close at hand, in these not so large islands, there is a hidden treasure, unknown to the vast majority of English-speaking people.

Is there something which unites the different times and different circumstances which lie behind these prayers and praises? Obviously, there is a common experience of, and faith in, the love of God revealed in Jesus Christ, imparted in the Holy Spirit. But that is something which links this tradition with the whole Christian world of which it is so clearly a part. Is there any special quality of vision or understanding which characterizes the spirituality of the Celtic peoples? We think that there is, and that is something which, despite all the differences, links the eighteenth-century farmer's wife in Wales with the ninth-century hermit in Ireland, a twentieth-century Quaker teacher with a thirteenth-century Franciscan friar.

What are these characteristics? First, there is an astonishing confidence that this world is God's world, that nature and grace belong together. Perhaps because the Celtic peoples were converted to Christianity very early, they received the gospel at a time when the Church was sure that the goodness of God healed and restored the whole of human nature and renewed the whole creation. But, as we have already noted, this love of the natural world, this confidence in God as Creator and as Redeemer does not make these people blind to the reality of evil, to the need for a radical repentance, to the elements of conflict in this world and in the life of each one. The cross is present here, but as in the high crosses of early Ireland, it is the cross of triumph, of the Christ who conquers through suffering.

Closely linked with these two basic points is a third, a powerful sense of the closeness of eternity to the things of every day. A modern Welsh poet declares that love of country involves 'keeping house amidst a cloud of witnesses'. The routine tasks of daily life are seen in an eternal perspective. Making a fire in the hearth is a job which links us with the mothering fire of the Spirit of God as it descends into our world, warming the frozen hearts of men and women into life. The angels and saints are not far away, and God's representatives are by no means always male. Indeed, 'there is a mother's heart in the heart of God'.

A sense of the sacredness of the earth and of all that grows on it, a sense that the victory of the cross illumines and transforms our life of every day, an awareness that heaven is not far from us, but that in our work and in our sleep we are accompanied by heavenly powers – these are some of the characteristics which appear in these pages. If there is a heightened awareness of the joy conveyed through our senses in the passages which celebrate the beauty of God's creation, there is no less powerful an awareness of the unrelenting pain and agony of the cross. In both joy and grief the body is involved together with the spirit.

All this is presented to us in a language full of vivid imagery. It is commonplace to say that it is the poetry which gets lost in the process of translation. But this is only partly true as the experience of the Christian centuries shows. Where would Christian prayer and worship be without the psalms of the Bible? Yet very few of us know Hebrew. Their power, their beauty, their depths and heights have come through translation into all the languages of Christendom. So it is, we hope, with the passages collected here. The sharpness and clarity of the originals, their preference for the language of image over that of abstract concept, comes through time and time again.

'In Eden, I shall always remember this, I lost blessings without number,/Down fell my bright crown', sings the eighteenth-century Methodist, William Williams, Pantycelyn, and the clarity and conciseness of his lines remind us of some of the earliest Irish poems. When the twentieth-century poet Euros Bowen sees the priest's eye straying from the celebration of the Eucharist to the hills and clouds outside the chapel and consecrating both, he links nature and grace in a common sacramental vision which reminds us of the hermits centuries before him. In prayer and praise the centuries are overpassed, and we late-twentieth-century urban people find our perceptions extended. So a proper concern for what is contemporary is opened out into the large room of the kingdom of eternity, the communion of saints.

The historical experience of the peoples represented in this book has often been that of suffering, oppression and defeat. The darker side of human existence has not passed them by. But through the power of their faith and the resilience of their song, the darkness has constantly been turned towards light. One of the greatest Irish poets of our time speaks of this sudden gift of illumination captured in the moment of a visit to a little early-Christian oratory on one of the headlands of Western Ireland. 'Inside, in the dark of the stone, it feels as if you are sustaining a great pressure, bowing down like the generations of monks who must have bowed down in meditation and reparation on the floor.' In such a place you feel 'the weight of Christianity in all its rebuking aspects, its calls to self-denial and self-abnegation, its humbling of the proud flesh and insolent spirit. But coming out of the cold heart of the stone into the sunlight and dazzle of grass and sea, I felt a lift in my heart, a surge towards happiness that must have been experienced over and over again by those monks as they crossed that same threshold centuries ago.' Here there is indeed 'a surge towards praise, a sudden apprehension of the world as light', an amazed recognition that heaven and earth alike are full of God's glory (Seamus Heaney, *Preoccupations, Selected Prose 1968–1978* (Faber 1980), p. 189).

A. M. ALLCHIN
ESTHER DE WAAL

*Notes* The sixty passages which follow are arranged in pairs. In each case a text from the Gaelic tradition (Irish or Scottish) on the left-hand page faces a text from the Welsh tradition on the right.

At the end of the book notes and references will be found. Here there is first a brief comment on each pair of texts, suggesting the themes which unify them; then references to the original sources are given. The figures in bold type refer to pages of the present book.

# I

## *Morning prayer*

I believe, O God of all gods,
That Thou art the eternal Father of life:
I believe, O God of all gods,
That Thou art the eternal Father of love.

I believe, O Lord and God of the peoples,
That Thou art the creator of the high heavens,
That Thou art the creator of the skies above,
That Thou art the creator of the oceans below.

I believe, O Lord and God of the peoples,
That Thou art He who created my soul and set
  its warp.
Who created my body from dust and from ashes,
Who gave to my body breath and to my soul its
  possession.

> Father, bless to me my body,
> Father, bless to me my soul,
> Father, bless to me my life,
> Father, bless to me my belief.

# I

## *Benediction*

Glorious Lord, I give you greeting!
Let the church and the chancel
    praise you,
Let the chancel and the church
    praise you,
Let the plain and the hillside praise
    you,
Let the world's three well-springs
    praise you,
Two above wind and one above land,
Let the dark and the daylight praise you.
Abraham, founder of the faith, praised you:
Let the life everlasting praise you,
Let the birds and honeybees praise you,
Let the shorn stems and the shoots praise you.
Both Aaron and Moses praised you:
Let the male and the female praise you,
Let the seven days and the stars praise you,
Let the air and the ether praise you,
Let the books and the letters praise you,
Let the fish in the swift streams praise you,
Let the thought and the action praise you,
Let the sand-grains and the earth-clods praise you,
Let all the good that's performed praise you.
And I shall praise you, Lord of glory:
Glorious Lord, I give you greeting!

## II

*Where is God? Where is God's dwelling?*

He has his dwelling around heaven and earth and sea and all that in them is. He inspires all, he quickens all, he dominates all, he supports all. He lights the light of the sun. He furnishes the light of the night. He has made springs in the dry land. He has set stars to minister to the greater lights.

. . . He is the God of heaven and earth, of sea and rivers, of sun and moon and stars, of the lofty mountains and the lowly valley, the God above heaven and under heaven.

# II

## *Praise*

Almighty Creator, who hast made all things,
The world cannot express all thy glories,
Even though the grass and the trees should sing.

The Father has wrought so great a multitude of
    wonders
That they cannot be equalled.
No letters can contain them, no letters can express
    them.

He who made the wonder of the world
Will save us, has saved us.
It is not too great toil to praise the Trinity.

Purely, humbly, in skilful verse
I should delight to give praise to the Trinity.

It is not too great toil to praise the Son of Mary.

# III

## *Encompassing prayer*

My Christ! my Christ! my shield, my encircler,
Each day, each night, each light, each dark:
>My Christ! my Christ! my shield, my
>encircler,
>Each day, each night, each light, each dark.

Be near me, uphold me, my treasure, my
triumph,
In my lying, in my standing, in my watching, in
my sleeping.

Jesus, Son of Mary! my helper, my encircler,
Jesus, Son of David! my strength everlasting:
>Jesus, Son of Mary! my helper, my encircler,
>Jesus, Son of David! my strength everlasting.

# III

## *Love divine, all loves excelling*

It is a flame of fire from midmost heaven that came down hither into the world, fire that will kindle my stubborn nature, fire that will fill my whole life; it will not fail while God remains in being.

I shall never be able to declare, if I should try as long as I live, how pleasant, how sweet, how strong his love is: it is an endless flame that came from midmost heaven to earth.

Thou hast kindled fire in me – the most perfect fire of heaven, which the great seas cannot quench at all.

O, a passionate, powerful strong flame of fire has been kindled in heaven; everlasting love it is, that has made a union between God and me.

## IV

## *The scribe in the woods*

The woodland thicket overtops me,
the blackbird sings me a lay, praise I will not
    conceal:
above my lined little booklet
the trilling of birds sings to me.

The clear cuckoo sings to me, lovely discourse,
in its grey cloak from the crest of the bushes;
truly – may the Lord protect me! –
well do I write under the forest wood.

# IV

## *The bright field*

I have seen the sun break through
to illuminate a small field
for a while, and gone my way
and forgotten it. But that was the pearl
of great price, the one field that had
the treasure in it. I realize now
that I must give all that I have
to possess it. Life is not hurrying

on to a receding future, nor hankering after
an imagined past. It is the turning
aside like Moses to the miracle
of the lit bush, to a brightness
that seemed as transitory as your youth
once, but is the eternity that awaits you.

# V

## *God with us*

A full household could not be more lovely than my little oratory in Tuaim Inbir with its stars in their order, with its sun and its moon.

That you may be told its story, it was a craftsman who made it – my little heart, God from Heaven, he is the thatcher who thatched it.

A house where rain does not pour, a place where spear-points are not dreaded, as bright as in a garden and with no fence about it.

# V

## The churches of Wales

There is our special heritage in Wales of hundreds and hundreds of little ancient churches. They are for the most part unknown, and come as a revelation to architects and lovers of the past who see them for the first time. They are quite different from any in England. They are small and simple and very much home-made. They fit the landscape and the climate; they are the offerings of a poor people, harassed over the centuries by war and living on land very different from the rich rolling counties of England. Only rarely do we see churches comparable to any of the great churches over the border and when we do, we find that they are the offerings of Englishmen and carried out by English masons . . . Because our idiom is so different it is apt to be despised.

The Welsh scale of things, the traditions, the achievements, should all be judged from a quite different level from England, for everything is on a smaller scale, and the very poverty, small size and simplicity of many of our churches is part and parcel of our heritage.

# VI

## *The hermit's song*

I have a hut in a wood: only my Lord knows it; an ash tree closes it on one side, and a hazel like a great tree by a rath on the other.

The size of my hut, small, not too small, a homestead with familiar paths. From its gable a she-bird sings a sweet song in her thrush's cloak.

A tree of apples of great bounty like a mansion, stout: a pretty bush, thick as a fist, of small hazelnuts, branching and green.

Fair white birds come, herons, seagulls, the sea sings to them, no mournful music: brown grouse from the russet heather.

The sound of the wind against a branching wood, grey cloud, riverfalls, the cry of the swan, delightful music!

Beautiful are the pines which make music for me unhindered: through Christ I am no worse off at any time than you.

Though you relish that which you enjoy exceeding all wealth, I am content with that which is given me by my gentle Christ.

With no moment of strife, no din of combat such as disturbs you, thankful to the Prince who gives every good to me in my hut.

# VI

## *The woodland Mass*

A pleasant place I was at today,
under mantles of the worthy green hazel,
listening at day's beginning
to the skilful cock thrush
singing a splendid stanza
of fluent signs and symbols;
about him was a setting
of flowers of the sweet boughs of May,
like green mantles, his chasuble
was of the wings of the wind.
There was here, by the great God,
nothing but gold in the altar's canopy.
I heard, in polished language,
a long and faultless chanting,
an unhesitant reading to the people
of a gospel without mumbling;
the elevation, on the hill for us there,
of a good leaf for a holy wafer.
Then the slim eloquent nightingale
from the corner of a grove nearby,
poetess of the valley, sings to the many
the Sanctus bell in lively whistling.
The sacrifice is raised
up to the sky above the bush,
devotion to God the Father,
the chalice of ecstasy and love.
The psalmody contents me:
it was bred of a birch-grove in the sweet woods.

# VII

## St Kevin and the blackbird

At one Lenten season, St Kevin, as was his way, fled from the company of men to a certain solitude, and in a little hut that did but keep out the sun and the rain, gave himself earnestly to reading and to prayer, and his leisure to contemplation alone. And as he knelt in his accustomed fashion, with his hand outstretched through the window and lifted up to heaven, a blackbird settled on it, and busying herself as in her nest, laid in it an egg. And so moved was the saint that in all patience and gentleness he remained, neither closing nor withdrawing his hand: but until the young ones were fully hatched he held it out unwearied, shaping it for the purpose.

# VII

## The fountain of creation

As with St John the Divine on the island of Patmos I was 'in the Spirit' and I had a vision, in which I could comprehend the breadth and length and depth and height of the mystery of the creation. But I won't try to put the experience into words. It would be impossible. I will simply say that I realized there was really no such thing as time, no beginning and no end but that everything is a fountain welling up endlessly from immortal God. There was certainly something in the place that gave me this feeling. The chapel stood in the fields, amidst the waving grass, its roof covered with a layer of yellow lichen. There were tall nettles growing around and at its side there swayed a big old tree like someone leaning forward to listen to the sermon. It was therefore easy to believe that I was living centuries ago. It might have been the first day of Creation and myself one of the first men. Might have been? No, it *was* the first day. The world was recreated before my eyes. The dew of its creation was on everything, and I fell to my knees and praised God – a young man worshipping a young God, for surely that is what our God is.

# VIII

## *A prayer for light*

Lord grant me, I pray thee in the name of Jesus Christ the Son, my God, that love which knows no fall so that my lamp may feel the kindling touch and know no quenching, may burn for me and for others may give light.

Do thou, Christ, deign to kindle our lamps, our Saviour most swc·t to us, that they may shine continually in thy temple, and receive perpetual light from thee the light perpetual, so that our darkness may be driven from us.

# VIII

## *Heaven on earth*

'It was as if lightning flashed into my spirit, and
I thought in my heart that the people around me
had seen it too, but they had not, and with the
light such a powerful peace and joy came into my
heart. In one moment I felt as if wholly revitalized
by some infinite power, so that my body would
be shattered like an earthen vessel. I saw God's
work in my soul and God's Word weaving
harmoniously together the peace which passes all
understanding, the exceeding greatness of His
power, etc. I could gladly seal with my blood the
truth of those words: Holy! Holy! Holy!
Wonderful! Wonderful! Eternally wonderful! I felt
as though my body and soul were being lifted
from the earth, and being dissolved to go to
heaven . . . Tears of joy flowed spontaneously
from my eyes in torrents . . . This lasted about
an hour or more as far as I can gauge. Indeed, it
lasted amazingly with me all that night; I could
neither eat nor drink; I felt a fullness within me.
If I slept it was but a little all night, I could only
praise and wonder at God, and who could do less?
Because it had become heaven to me on earth;
thank God from my heart! . . . I cannot reckon it
as one of the days of earth, only as one of the
days of heaven.'

# IX

## *Be thou my vision*

Be thou my vision, beloved Lord: none other is aught but the King of the seven heavens.

Be thou my meditation by day and night: may it be thou that I behold for ever in my sleep.

Be thou my speech: be thou my understanding: be thou for me: may I be for thee.

Be thou my father: may I be thy son: mayst thou be mine: may I be thine.

Be thou alone my special love: let there be none other save the High-King of heaven.

Thy love in my soul and in my heart – grant this to me, O King of the seven heavens.

Beloved Christ, whate'er befall me, O Ruler of all, be thou my vision.

# IX

## *Day by day*

Dear sister, I see more need than ever to spend my remaining days in giving myself up daily and continually, body and soul, into the care of him who is able to keep that which is committed to him against that day. Not to give myself once, but to live continually giving myself, right up to and in the very moment when I put away this tabernacle. Dear sister, the thought of putting it away is particularly sweet sometimes; I can say that this is what cheers me more than anything else in these days, not death in itself, but the great gain that is to be got through it. To be able to leave behind every inclination that goes against the will of God, to leave behind every ability to dishonour the law of God, with all weakness swallowed up by strength, to become fully conformed to the law which is already on one's heart and to enjoy God's likeness for ever. Dear sister, I am sometimes absorbed so far into these things that I completely fail to stand in the way of my duty with regard to temporal things, but I look for the time when I may find release and be with Christ, for that is much better, although it is very good here through a lattice, and the Lord sometimes reveals through a glass, darkly, as much of his glory as my weak faculties can bear.

# X

## *Blessing of the kindling*

I will kindle my fire this morning
In the presence of the holy angels of heaven,
In the presence of Ariel of the loveliest form,
In the presence of Uriel of the myriad charms,
Without malice, without jealousy, without envy,
Without fear, without terror of anyone under the
   sun,
But the Holy Son of God to shield me.
   Without malice, without jealousy, without
      envy,
   Without fear, without terror of anyone under
      the sun,
   But the Holy Son of God to shield me.

God, kindle Thou in my heart within
A flame of love to my neighbour,
To my foe, to my friend, to my kindred all,
To the brave, to the knave, to the thrall,
O Son of the loveliest Mary,
From the lowliest thing that liveth,
To the Name that is highest of all.

# X

## *Invocation*

We call her now to walk on the riverbank,
Brigid of Ireland, Ffraed of Wales, the Saint, the
  golden one,
who breaks the ice, dipping first one hand, then
  two hands,
freeing the river to flow into time of seed,
time of ripening, time of harvest.
We greet her from her churches and her wells,
from the cold sea-coast and the doorsteps of hill
  farms,
with the immemorial cry,
'Ffraed is come! Ffraed is welcome!'

We call you, saint of fire,
Protectress of the peat-stack,
meet us where we kneel on the hearth.
Give kind warmth of fire
to us and our kin,
like the outstretched hands of a mother
taking our hands,
like her arms sheltering us.
Be in the midst of the house,
be the mothering fire
in the midst of the house.

# XI

## *God our Mother*

There is a mother's heart in the heart of God.

# XI

## *A Christian woman*

'Think of your mother,' said he. 'Did you ever meet anyone who knew so much suffering? And yet did anyone enjoy more true happiness? Where did it spring from? From looking into herself? Not a bit of it! She had learnt to look on One who is worth looking at. I always felt that the greater her trials, the greater was her joy. Her poverty only made her mind dwell on the riches which are in Christ . . . Don't take offence, now, but the fact is that whenever I heard that your mother was in trouble, I would laugh and say, "Well, this is another feast for Mary Lewis!" . . . Never in my life did I see anyone who could live so completely as she could on the resources of her religion.'

# XII

## *St Ide's wish*

'I will take nothing from my Lord,' said she, 'unless He gives me His Son from Heaven in the form of a baby to be nursed by me' . . . So that Christ came to her in the form of a baby, and she said then:

'Little Jesus, Who is nursed by me in my little hermitage – even a priest with store of wealth, all is false but little Jesus.

The nursing which I nurse in my house is not the nursing of any base churl, Jesus with the folk of Heaven at my heart every single night.

Little young Jesus, my everlasting good, gives and is not remiss; the King Who has power over all, not to pray to Him will be repented.

It is Jesus, noble and angelic, not a paltry priest, Who is nursed by me in my little hermitage; Jesus the son of the Jewess.

Sons of princes, sons of kings, though they come to my land, not from them do I expect any good, I prefer little Jesus.'

# XII

## *Carol*

On this day's morn, a little child, a little child,
The root of Jesse was born, a little child.
The Mighty One from Bozra
The Lawgiver on Mount Sinai
The Atonement won on Calvary, a little child, a
little child,
Sucking at Mary's breast, a little child.

The living waters of Ezekiel, on Mary's knee, on
Mary's knee.
The wise child of Isaiah,
The promise given to Adam,
The Alpha and Omega, on Mary's knee, on
Mary's knee,
In a stall in Bethlehem Judah, on Mary's knee.

Christ put aside his crown, of his free will, of his
free will,
That Zion might be crowned, of his free will,
To bow his undefiled head,
Beneath the mocking crown of thorns,
To suffer angry scorn, of his free will, of his free
will,
To raise the guilty's head, of his free will.

# XIII

## *Christmas carol*

This night is the long night,
It will snow and it will drift,
White snow there will be till day,
White moon there will be till morn,
This night is the eve of the Great Nativity,
This night is born Mary Virgin's Son,
This night is born Jesus, Son of the King of glory,
This night is born to us the root of our joy,
This night gleamed the sun of the mountains high,
This night gleamed sea and shore together,
This night was born Christ the King of greatness
Ere it was heard that the Glory was come,
Heard was the wave upon the strand,
Ere 'twas heard that His foot had reached the
  earth,
Heard was the song of the angels glorious,
This night is the long night.

# XIII

## *Word made flesh*

Let us weigh wisely, let us wonder
    at
        Wonders accomplished,
Nothing more wondrous in this
    world ever
        Will men's lips tell of,
God coming to us, He that created
        All of creation,
As God and as man, and God as a
    man,
        Equally gifted.
Tremendous,    tiny,    powerful,
    feeble,
        Cheeks fair of colour,
Wealthy and needy, Father and
    Brother,
        Maker of brothers,
This, sure, is Jesus, whom we should welcome
        As Lord of rulers,
Lofty and lowly, Emmanuel,
        Honey to think on.
An ox and an ass, the Lord of this world,
        A manger is His,
Bundle of hay instead of a cradle
        For our Lord of hosts.

# XIV

## *Christ's cross*

Christ's cross over this face, and thus over my ear. Christ's cross over this eye. Christ's cross over this nose.

Christ's cross to accompany me before. Christ's cross to accompany me behind me. Christ's cross to meet every difficulty both on hollow and hill.

Christ's cross eastwards facing me. Christ's cross back towards the sunset. In the north, in the south, increasingly may Christ's cross straightway be.

Christ's cross up to broad Heaven. Christ's cross down to earth. Let no evil or hurt come to my body or my soul.

Christ's cross over me as I sit. Christ's cross over me as I lie. Christ's cross be all my strength until we reach the King of Heaven.

From the top of my head to the nail of my foot, O Christ, against every danger I trust in the protection of the cross.

Till the day of my death, going into this clay, I shall draw without – Christ's cross over this face.

# XIV

## *Conversion*

June 18th, 1735, being in secret prayer, I felt suddenly my heart melting within me like wax before the fire with love to God my Saviour; and also felt not only love, peace, etc., but longing to be dissolved, and to be with Christ; then was a cry in my inmost soul, which I was totally unacquainted with before, Abba Father! Abba Father! I could not help calling God my Father; I knew that I was his child, and that He loved me, and heard me. My soul being filled and satiated, crying, ''Tis enough, I am satisfied. Give me strength, and I will follow thee through fire and water.' I could say I was happy indeed! There was in me a well of water, springing up to everlasting life (John 4:14). The love of God was shed abroad in my heart by the Holy Ghost (Rm 5:5).

# XV

## *The cross*

They offered him a parting drink, desiring that he should die soon; an unlawful deed, they mixed gall with vinegar for him.

He raised a soft reproachful voice, beseeching his holy father: 'Why, O living God, hast Thou left me to my servitude and my suffering?'

The sun concealed its proper light; it lamented its lord. A swift cloud went across the blue sky, the great stormy sea roared.

The whole world became dark, great trembling came on the earth; at the death of noble Jesus great rocks burst open.

Jerusalem suddenly cast up the dead from ancient burial; in the hour in which Jesus suffered death the veil of the temple was rent.

A fierce stream of blood boiled until the bark of every tree was red; there was blood throughout the world in the tops of every great wood.

It would have been fitting for God's elements – the fair sea, the blue sky, the earth – to have changed their appearance, lamenting their calamity.

The body of Christ exposed to the spear-thrust demanded harsh lamentation – that they should have mourned more grievously the Man by whom they were created.

# XV

## *He who was on the cross*

That word is on my mind tonight, 'Go forth, O
ye daughters of Zion, and behold king Solomon
with the crown wherewith his mother crowned
him in the day of his espousals, and in the day of
the gladness of his heart.' I think there is a high
and peculiar calling for all who have part in the
covenant to leave their own ceiled houses to see
their King wearing the crown of thorns and the
purple robe. No wonder the sun hid its rays when
its creator was pierced by nails. It is a marvel to
me to think who it is that was on the cross, he
whose eyes are as a flame of fire piercing through
heaven and earth in a single glance, unable to see
his creatures, the work of his hands. My mind is
too overwhelmed to say anything more on the
matter.

# XVI

## *The crucifixion*

At the cry of the first bird
They began to crucify Thee,
O cheek like a swan,
It were not right ever to cease
    lamenting –
It was like the parting of day
    from night.

Ah! though sore the suffering
Put upon the body of Mary's Son –
Sorer to Him was the grief
That was upon her for His sake.

# XVI

## *To the good thief*

You did not see Him on the mount of the
    Transfiguration
    Nor the night He walked the sea;
You never saw corpses colour when bier and
    grave
    Felt the force of His cry.

You did not hear the parables shaped like a
    Parthenon of language,
    Nor His tone in talking of His Father,
Neither did you hear the secrets of the upper
    room,
    Nor the prayer before Cedron and betrayal.

O master of courtesy and manners, who
    enlightened for you
    Your part in the savage charade?
'Lord, when you come to your kingdom,
    remember me,' –
    The kingdom conquered through dying.

O thief who stole Paradise from the nails of a
    stake,
    Marshal of heaven's nobility,
Pray that we before the hour of our death have
    the gift
    To see Him and know Him.

# XVII

## *Christ's bounties*

. . . O Son of God, do a miracle for me, and change my heart; Thy having taken flesh to redeem me was more difficult than to transform my wickedness.

It is Thou who, to help me, didst go to be scourged by the Jews; Thou, dear child of Mary, art the refined molten metal of our forge.

It is Thou who makest the sun bright, together with the ice; it is Thou who createst the rivers and the salmon all along the river.

That the nut-tree should be flowering, O Christ, it is a rare craft; through Thy skill too comes the kernel, Thou fair ear of our wheat.

Though the children of Eve ill deserve the bird-flocks and the salmon, it was the Immortal One on the cross who made both salmon and birds.

It is He who makes the flower of the sloes grow through the surface of the blackthorn, and the nut-flower on other trees; beside this, what miracle is greater?

# XVII

## *Death and life have contended*

In Eden – I shall always remember this –
I lost blessings numberless as the dew;
   Down fell my bright crown:
But the victory of Calvary
Won them back for me again;
   I shall sing as long as I live.

Faith! yonder is the place, and yonder the tree,
On which the Prince of heaven was nailed,
   Innocent, in my place;
The dragon has been crushed by the One;
As two were wounded, One has conquered,
   And that One was Jesus.

# XVIII

## *Hermit prayer*

O Son of the living God, old eternal King, I desire a hidden hut in the wilderness that it may be my home.

A narrow little blue stream beside it and a clear pool for the washing away of sin through the grace of the Holy Ghost.

A lovely wood close about it on every side, to nurse birds with all sorts of voices and to hide them with its shelter.

Looking south for heat, and a stream through its land, and good fertile soil suitable for all plants.

A beautiful draped church, a home for God from Heaven, and bright lights above the clean white Gospels.

Enough of clothing and food from the King of fair fame, and to be sitting for a while and praying to God in every place.

# XVIII

## *Reredos*

The reredos was not
an ecclesiastical adornment
of symbols,
but plain glass,
with the danger
of distracting the celebrant
from
the properties of the communion table,

for
in the translucence
the green earth
budded in the morning view,
the river was in bloom,
the air a joyous flight,
and the sunshine
set the clouds ablaze,

and I noticed
the priest's eyes
as it were unconsciously
placing his hand
on these gifts,
as though these
were
the bread and the wine.

# XIX

## *Peace*

The peace of God, the peace of men,
The peace of Columba kindly,
   Mary mild, the loving
   Christ, king of tenderness,
The peace of Christ, king of tenderness.

Be upon each window, upon each door,
Upon each hole that lets in light,
Upon the four corners of my house,
Upon the four corners of my bed,
   Upon the four corners of my bed.

Upon each thing my eye takes in,
Upon each thing my mouth takes in,
Upon my body that is of earth,
And upon my soul that came from on high,
   Upon my body that is of earth,
   And upon my soul that came from on high.

# XIX

## *St David (1)*

There is no barrier between two worlds in the
    Church,
The Church militant on earth
Is one with the Church triumphant in heaven,
And the saints are in this Church which is two in
    one.
They come to worship with us, our small
    congregation,
The saints our oldest ancestors
Who built Wales on the foundation
Of the Crib, the Cross and the Empty Tomb.
And they go out as before to travel their old ways
And to evangelize Wales.
I have seen Dewi going from shire to shire like
    the gipsy of God.
With the gospel and the altar in his caravan;
He came to us in the colleges and schools
To show us the purpose of learning.
He went down into the pit with the coal miners
And shone his lamp on to the coal face.
He put on the goggles of the steel worker, and
    the short grey overall.
And showed the Christian being purified like
    metal in the furnace.

# XX

## *The heavenly banquet*

I would like to have the men of Heaven
In my own house:
With vats of good cheer
Laid out for them.

I would like to have the three Marys,
Their fame is so great.
I would like people
From every corner of Heaven.

I would like them to be cheerful
In their drinking,
I would like to have Jesus too
Here amongst them.

I would like a great lake of beer
For the King of Kings,
I would like to be watching Heaven's family
Drinking it through all eternity.

## St David (2)

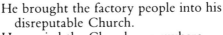

He brought the factory people into his
  disreputable Church.
He carried the Church everywhere
Like a body with life and mind and
  will,
And he did things small and great.
He brought the Church into our
  homes,
Put the holy vessels on the kitchen
  table
With bread from the pantry and wine
  from the cellar,
And he stood behind the table like a
  tramp
So as not to hide from us the wonder of the
  sacrifice.
And after the Communion we had a talk round
  the fire
And he spoke to us of God's natural order,
The person, the family, the nation and the society
  of nations
And the cross which prevents us from making
  any of them into a god.
He said that God had made our nation
For his own purposes
And that its death would be a breach of that
  order . . .

# XXI

## *The hermit's life*

All alone in my little hut without any human being in my company, dear has been the pilgrimage before going to meet death.

Making holy the body with good habits, treading it boldly down: feeble tearful eyes for forgiveness of my passions.

Stepping along the paths of the gospel, singing psalms every hour: an end of talking and long stories: constant bending of the knee.

My Creator to frequent me, my Lord, my King, my spirit to seek him in the eternal kingdom where he is.

All alone in my little hut, all alone so, alone I came into the world, alone I shall go from it.

# XXI

## *Thirsting after heaven*

It is the view of this that increases eternal life in
our souls, and makes us become as pilgrims on the
earth, and go on cheerfully towards the heavenly
Jerusalem. My dear sister, there is an ocean of
happiness prepared for us; and what we experience
here is but a drop, or a taste of that which we
shall enjoy. A sight of his love is the cause of our
love; and our thirst after him is but the effect of
his thirst after us; and our diligence in seeking of
him is the effect of his diligence in seeking of us.
A sight of this will break our heart and make us
look upon ourselves as nothing in his sight.

# XXII

## *Three kinds of martyrdom*

Now there are three kinds of martyrdom which are counted as a cross to man, that is to say, white martyrdom, and green martyrdom, and red martyrdom.

This is the white martyrdom to man, when he separates for the sake of God from everything he loves, although he suffer fasting or labour thereat.

This is the green martyrdom to him, when by means of them (fasting and penance) he separates from his desires, or suffers toil in penance and repentance.

This is the red martyrdom to him, endurance of a cross or destruction for Christ's sake, as has happened to the apostles in the persecution of the wicked and in teaching the law of God.

These three kinds of martyrdom are comprised in the carnal ones who resort to good repentance, who separate from their desires, who pour forth their blood in fasting and in labour for Christ's sake.

# XXII

## *Praise of the martyrs*

After the silent centuries I weave their praise.
The core of faith is one and it is splendid to know
Souls that are one with the quick in the root of
  Being.

They are one with the light. They are above my
  head
Where, through the expanse, peace gathers.
When the sky turns to night
Each one is for my eye a rent in the veil.

The light-footed runners, we cannot count them
  all,
Gathering in a company above the pit of
  perdition.
Surely nothing can scatter them, who all paid the
  same toll.

The quiet final payment. Giving a world for a
  world,
Giving the utmost torment for the guidance of the
  Spirit,
Giving the flower for the root, and placing a grain
  in its cradle.

The disembowelling after the hurdle of torture,
  and before
The groaning where their souls were given a
  ladder to ascend

To the broad next morning of the Golgotha of
  their blessed Lord.

# XXIII

## *Mary, mother of us all*

I wrap my soul and my body within
   Under thy guarding this night, O Bride,
   Calm Nurse-mother to Christ without sin,
Calm Nurse-mother to the Christ's wounded side.

I wrap my soul and my body so sure
   'Neath thy guarding this night, Mary dear,
   Tender Mother of Christ of sorrow's tear.

I wrap my soul and my body from fears
   Under thy guarding, O Christ, this night,
   Thou pierced Son of the wounds, the tears,
May thy cross this night be shielding aright.

I wrap my soul and my body so sure
   Under thy guarding, O God, this night,
   Aid-Father to feeble pilgrims poor,
Protector of earth and heav'n in might,
   Earth and heav'n's Protector in might.

# XXIII

## *Angharad*

For many was her concern
At nightfall, and she rejoiced with many too,
Sensing the pain, joining the feast,
In the ocean of her heart was cherishing.
To her doors the troubled came
The weary knew the way to her court.
Angharad wore a scarlet gown
Down to her feet; it was made of good works.

She bore the turmoil of the fragile heart
Through her encouragement overcoming fears.
On her knees in the early morning
She gave her day to the Kingdom,
Giving the simplicity of her today
As wine to the King, and to the wound.
Caring for his riches
She recreated with her praise an unblemished
world . . .

Anger and jealousy she broke
Healing with fruits of her tree;
Freely extending the generous gift . . .
She gave to God from the two aspects
Pain and joy in harmony.
She gives to us in the Spirit of the Lord
The priesthood of her concern.

# XXIV

## *The blessing of the Trinity*

In name of Father,
In name of Son,
In name of Spirit,
  Three in One:

Father cherish me,
Son cherish me,
Spirit cherish me,
  Three all-kindly.

God make me holy,
Christ make me holy,
Spirit make me holy,
  Three all-holy.

Three aid my hope,
Three aid my love,
Three aid mine eye,
  And my knee from stumbling,
  My knee from stumbling.

# XXIV

## *The indwelling of God*

I finde that the Lord Jesus is as a golden Mine in our owne fields, under our owne earth, and is in Saints as the soul in the eye, or Sun in the Firmament, or fire in the inward furnace, or inhabitant in a house. But O! how few see that the very same Son, in whom the three is in one, is in Saints, though the Scripture be not afraid to say, that the Trinity is in all Saints.

# XXV

## *Prayer for protection*

Be the eye of God dwelling with you,
The foot of Christ in guidance with you,
The shower of the Spirit pouring on you,
Richly and generously.

# XXV

## *New life*

The water of baptism is the fresh growth of the
    world
And is called the fount of the healing oil of faith.

# XXVI

## St Columba at Iona

Delightful I think it to be in the bosom of an isle
on the crest of a rock,
that I may see often
the calm of the sea.

That I may see its heavy waves
over the glittering ocean
as they chant a melody to their Father
on their eternal course.

That I may see its ebb and its flood-tide
in its flow;
that this should be my name, a secret I declare,
'He who turned his back on Ireland.'

That I may bless the Lord
who has power over all,
heaven with its crystal orders of angels,
earth, ebb, flood-tide.

That I may pore on one of my books,
good for my soul,
a while kneeling for beloved heaven,
a while at psalms.

A while meditating upon the Prince of Heaven.

# XXVI

## *Wales*

Martyrs' dust through countless ages
  And the saints lie in thy breast,
Thou didst give them breath and being,
  Thou didst call them to thy rest.

On thy roads are seen the footprints
  Made by angels from above,
And the Holy Ghost has settled
  In thy branches like a dove.

Bards have heard in winds and breezes
  Sighs of sacrificial pain,
Deep within thy darkest forests
  The Rood Tree doth still remain.

His Resurrection was thy springtime,
  Thy summer was His triumph green,
And in the winter of thy mountains
  Tabernacles have been seen.

Providential dews and raindrops
  On thy fields of oat and corn,
And his Glory on the harness
  Of thy horses in the morn.

Thy saints are clothed in morning radiance,
  They love thee, thy joy and pride, –
Like a mother-bird thou callest,
  Warm beneath thy wing they hide.

# XXVII

## *Joyous death*

Give Thou to me, O God,
The death of the priceless oil;
Give Thou to me, O God,
That the Healer of my soul be near me;
Give Thou to me, O God,
The death of joy and of peace.

Give Thou to me, O God,
To confess the death of Christ;
Give Thou to me, O God,
To meditate the agony of Christ;
Give Thou to me, O God,
To make warm the love of Christ.

O great God of Heaven,
Draw Thou my soul to Thyself
That I may make repentance
With a right and a strong heart,
With a heart broken and contrite,
That shall not change nor bend nor yield.

O great God of the angels,
Bring Thou me to the dwelling of peace;
O great God of the angels,
Preserve me from the evil of the fairies;
O great God of the angels,
Bathe me in the bathing of Thy pool.

# XXVII

## *Prayer on his death-bed*

I salute God, asylum's gift,
To praise my Lord, bounteous, benign,
Sole Son of Mary, source of morn and eve
And teeming river-mouths,
Who made wood, and mead, and true measure,
And harvests, and God's overflowing gifts,
Who made grass and grove and mountain heather,
Made one man joyful, righteous judgement,
And another in need, ungifted,
Impoverished and bitter-tempered.
I pray God's Son, for He has power,
To forgive our sin, sinning is wrong,
And welcome us in heaven's haven:
May we go to the land we long for.
And He, heaven's Lord, portion of peace,
Brought us forth from perdition when pierced,
And He rose for us, and won His reward,
And the Lord will not deny us His help.

# XXVIII

## *Pilgrimage*

To go to Rome
Is much trouble, little profit.
The King whom thou seekest there,
Unless thou bring Him with thee, thou wilt not
find.

# XXVIII

## *Journey without end*

Thy beauty will be ever new, ever freshly kindling a fire, through all the ages of eternity, evermore without fail; a fervent flame without end, through all the degrees of heaven together, it will continue to burn brightly as long as God himself shall last. There is nothing in heaven or on earth but thy divine greatness that could kindle such love as I now feel; who could settle my unquiet spirit, who could establish me in my place, but He, the Illimitable, who is the perfection of earth and heaven?

Yonder there is no end of singing, yonder there is no end of praise, yonder there is no end of remembering every past trouble; never will it cease, the praise of God in our Father's house. A beginning of song, a beginning of praise – such, O Jesus, at the end of a thousand long ages, will be the joy of the pilgrims yonder at the end of their road; there will never be an end to the sound of the golden harp.

# XXIX

## *Angels*

The maker of all things,
The Lord God worship we:
Heaven white with angels' wings,
Earth and the white-waved sea.

# XXIX

## *Saints*

Bright, bright
The fellowship of saints in light,
Far, far beyond all earthly sight.
No plague can blight, no foe destroy.
United here they live in love:
O then, above how deep their joy!

Set free
By Jesu's mortal wounds are we,
Blest with rich gifts – and more shall be.
Blessings has he in endless store:
Some drops are showered upon us here;
What when we hear the ocean's roar?

Deep, deep
The feast of life and peace they keep
In that fair world beyond death's sleep.
Our hearts will leap their joys to see
Who, with the Lamb's dear merits graced,
All sorrow past, reign glad and free.

# XXX

## *The guiding light*

O God, who broughtest me from the rest of last
   night
Unto the joyous light of this day
Be Thou bringing me from the new light of this
   day
Unto the guiding light of eternity.
   Oh! from the new light of this day
   Unto the guiding light of eternity.

# XXX

## *Darkness tends towards light*

I see the black cloud
　　Now about to flee,
And the wind from the north
　　Is veering just a little;
After a great storm, there will shortly come
Pleasant weather upon my poor soul.

Nothing will remain long
　　Of the black stormy night;
Long ages have not been appointed
　　For anyone to carry the cross;
The glad dawn that shines yonder
Says that a fine morning is on the way.

I see the sunlight
　　On the hills of my Father's house,
Showing me the foundation
　　Of my free salvation;
That my name is up there on the books of heaven,
And that there is nothing that can blot it out.

Sweet as the honeycomb,
　　And nourishing and healing,
Are all heaven's chastisements
　　And the strokes of my Father's rod:
Each cross, each woe, each strong wind
Ripens saints for heaven.

# Notes

## I

Here is worship with all human capacities, with and for the whole of humanity, and the whole of creation. This coinherence of the universe and humankind is a common theme throughout the Celtic approach to God.

**20** This morning prayer comes from Mary Gillies, a crofter in the Outer Hebrides. It is part of the oral tradition of Gaelic songs and blessings which were selected at the end of the nineteenth century by Alexander Carmichael and published as *Carmina Gadelica, Hymns and Incantations with Illustrative Notes of Words, Rites and Customs Dying and Obsolete*: Orally collected in the Highlands and Islands of Scotland by Alexander Carmichael (Edinburgh, Scottish Academic Press), 6 vols. from 1900. This extract comes from vol. iii, pp. 45–7.

**21** Joseph P. Clancy, *The Earliest Welsh Poetry* (Macmillan 1970), p. 113. A poem from the eleventh century. All things praise God: birds, beasts, elements; men and women, books and thoughts, church and chancel.

## II

There is a sense of the indwelling of the Creator in all things, focused in the Christ. The Holy Spirit is creative and life-giving in the world and in human faith.

**22** A legend tells of the encounter between St Patrick

and two princesses who questioned him about the Christian faith. A dialogue ensued which took the form of a catechism, and the extract gives two of the saint's replies. Leslie Hardinge, *The Celtic Church in Britain* (SPCK 1972), p. 104.

**23** Ifor Williams, *The Beginnings of Welsh Poetry* (University of Wales Press 1972), p. 102. A Welsh poem written in the margin of a ninth-century Latin manuscript (translation adapted).

## III

The deepest human needs and longings, pre-Christian as well as Christian, are met by the encompassing love of God which descends into the world, surrounding and penetrating us.

**24** From Alexander Macdonald, crofter, Barra, *Carmina Gadelica*, op. cit., p. 77.

**25** *Llyfr Emynau a Thonau* (Caernarfon 1929), 80, v. 2; 192, v. 2; 157, v. 1; 80, v. 2. Selected verses from the greatest Welsh hymn-writer, William Williams, Pantycelyn (1716–91).

## IV

This is not just nature poetry, but nature poetry transfigured; all things seen through eyes washed clean by prayer and love.

**26** Kenneth Jackson, *Studies in Early Celtic Nature Poetry* (Cambridge 1935), p. 3. Eighth- or ninth-century.

**27** R. S. Thomas, *Laboratories of the Spirit* (Macmillan 1975), p. 60. R. S. Thomas, the outstanding poet in English in Wales today. Formerly Vicar of Aberdaron, Gwynedd.

# V

Inconspicuous parish churches still bear the name of the one who founded them, and still give shelter to the human heart. They remind us of the simplicity and secrecy of God's presence.

**28** This is all that remains of a ninth-century lyric by an Irish monastic poet. David Greene and Frank O'Connor (eds.), *A Golden Treasury of Irish Poetry*, AD *600–1200* (Macmillan 1967), p. 101.
**29** Owain W. Jones, *Glyn Simon, His Life and Opinions* (Gomer Press 1981), p. 78. From an address given by Glyn Simon when he was Archbishop of Wales.

# VI

The hermit joys in his natural surroundings; the court poet sees the wood in springtime as a kind of liturgy.

**30** *Early Irish Lyrics, Eighth to Twelfth Century*, ed. Gerard Murphy (Oxford 1956), pp. 11–19, shortened. Tenth-century.
**31** Gwyn Williams, *Introduction to Welsh Poetry* (Faber 1953), pp. 49–50. Part of a poem by Dafydd ap Gwilym (*c.* 1320–1380), commonly regarded as the greatest Welsh poet.

# VII

Ecstasy in creation leads to infinite care and gentleness in the handling of created things in all their forms.

**32** St Kevin and the blackbird; Giraldus Cambrensis, *Topographia Hibernica*, ii: 28. Trans. Helen Waddell, *Beasts and Saints* (Constable 1934), p. 137.

**33** R. S. Thomas, *Selected Prose* (Poetry Wales Press 1983), p. 44. Translated from an early article in Welsh describing a visit to two chapels in mid-Wales.

## VIII

The presence of God and the love of God are focused in the light which shines from the face of Jesus Christ.

**34** A prayer of St Columbanus. Michael Maher (ed.), *Irish Spirituality* (Dublin, Veritas Publications 1981), p. 14.
**35** The experience is that of John Thomas, a Camarthenshire Methodist. It took place on 2 March 1757. Eifion Evans, *Daniel Rowland and the Great Evangelical Awakening in Wales* (Banner of Truth Trust 1985), pp. 292–3.

## IX

The vision of eternity has to be realized and appropriated day by day in the constant demands and uncertainties of ordinary life.

**36** A lorica, or breastplate. Shortened. The full version can be found in Murphy, op. cit., pp. 43–4.
**37** From one of the letters of Ann Griffiths (1776–1805), a farmer's wife in Montgomeryshire. The most theological of Welsh hymn-writers. Trans. H. A. Hodges. A. M. Allchin, *Ann Griffiths* (University of Wales Press 1976), p. 54.

## X

The flame of love which warms and feeds at the centre of the household is needed in all our lives, bringing light and warmth into the dark times of the year, and our own dark places.

**38** When 'lifting' the fire in the rhorning the woman prays, in an undertone, that the fire may be blessed to her and to her household, and to the glory of God who gave it. The people look upon the fire as a miracle of divine power provided for their good – to warm their bodies when they are cold, to cook their food when they are hungry, and to remind them that they too, like the fire, need constant renewal mentally and physically. *Carmina Gadelica*, vol. i, p. 231.

**39** From a broadcast poem by Ruth Bidgood, published in the *Anglo-Welsh Review* (1981). St Brigid of Kildare is known as St Bride or St Ffraed in Wales. A saint around whom much legend has gathered.

## XI

When the human heart is open to the heart of God, then the totality of the divine loving becomes accessible to uphold and sustain us.

**40** Hebridean saying, Alistair Maclean, *Hebridean Altars*, quoted by Martin Reith, *God in our Midst, Prayers and Devotions from Northern Scotland* (SPCK 1975), p. 5.

**41** D. M. and E. M. Lloyd, *A Book of Wales* (Collins 1953), pp. 366–7, from a novel by Daniel Owen (1836–95), the outstanding Welsh-language novelist of the nineteenth century.

## XII

The ties of mother and child are simply an expression of the intimacy that all of us, men as well as women, can feel at Christ's closeness to us.

**42** St Ide's wish; probably ninth-century. Kenneth

Jackson, *A Celtic Miscellany, Translations from the Celtic Literatures* (Routledge & Kegan Paul 1951), pp. 312–13.
**43** Verses taken from a traditional carol still sung at Christmastime in the Tanat Valley in Montgomeryshire.

# XIII

The paradoxes of faith are celebrated in different ways, in the timeless, flowing quality of a Hebridean carol, and in the intricate meditation of a Franciscan friar.

**44** This Christmas carol from Roderick MacNeill, cottar of Barra, is given here without the refrain that follows each line. Christmas chants were numerous and on Christmas Eve bands of young men went about from house to house chanting Christmas songs. *Carmina Gadelica*, op. cit., vol. iii, pp. 111–13.
**45** Part of a poem by Madawg ap Gwallter, Franciscan friar, (*fl.* 1250). Joseph P. Clancy, *The Earliest Welsh Poetry* (Macmillan 1970), p. 163.

# XIV

The first moments of the experience of the power of Christ's cross are to grow into a continuing awareness of his ever-present strength and support.

**46** This is one of the many versions of the Irish 'breast-plate' tradition, of which St Patrick's breastplate is the most familiar. Gerard Murphy, op. cit., pp. 33–4.
**47** This extract comes from the diary of Howell Harris (1714–73), one of the leading figures in Welsh Methodism. It comes from 18 June 1735, a few weeks after his conversion experience at Holy Communion in Talgarth parish church. Eifion Evans, op. cit., p. 51.

## XV

In the suffering of God all creation is involved and transformed. The sense of the cross as a universal mystery runs through the whole tradition.

**48** Blathmacc, an eighth-century Irish poet, retold the biblical story in long narrative poems. His work has the interest of belonging to the movement that produced the great scriptural crosses. David Green and Frank O'Connor (eds.), *A Golden Treasury of Irish Poetry, AD 600–1200* (Macmillan 1967), p. 42.

**49** A. M. Allchin, *Ann Griffiths* (University of Wales Press 1976), p. 52. From a letter of Ann to John Hughes, Pontrobert. Our own 'ceiled houses' are the little worlds of our own theories and imaginations which we have to transcend if we are to see the true glory of the cross.

## XVI

God's light reveals nature to us as beautiful; it also reveals the suffering and agony of the world in its extreme physical expressions. Just as the body and the senses convey joy, so they render us vulnerable to pain.

**50** *Selections from Ancient Irish Poetry*. Trans. Kuno Meyer (Constable 1911, new ed. 1959), p. 99.

**51** Joseph P. Clancy, *Twentieth-century Welsh Poems* (Gomer Press 1982), p. 78. Translated from the poem of Saunders Lewis (1893–1985), the greatest Welsh writer of our time, a convert to Roman Catholicism.

## XVII

The Creator is nailed to the tree of the cross, and thereby frees his universe and each one of us, from the power of destruction. The tree in the garden which brought death has become the tree on the hill which brings life.

**52** Irish, fifteenth-century. K. H. Jackson, *A Celtic Miscellany*, op. cit., pp. 329–30.
**53** *Llyfr Emynau a Thonau* (Caernarfon 1929), 216. William Williams, Pantycelyn. One of the greatest and best loved of his hymns.

# XVIII

There is no separation between the inner and the outer; the gifts on the altar and the gifts of the universe. Their common source is perceived by eyes and hands alike.

**54** A tenth-century poem attributed to St Manchon. David Greene and Frank O'Connor (eds.), op. cit., p. 150.
**55** Euros Bowen, *Detholion* (Yr Academi Cymreig 1984), p. 199. Euros Bowen (1904–    ), the outstanding poet writing in Welsh today. For many years Rector of Llangywer on the shores of Lake Bala. Author's translation.

# XIX

Heaven and earth are very close, and the angels and saints surround us. The sacred is secular and the secular is sacred.

**56** *Carmina Gadelica*, op. cit., vol. iii, p. 265.
**57** Gwenallt, *Eples* (Gomer Press 1951), pp. 63–4. This and **59** come from a poem by D. Gwenallt Jones (1899–1968). Both passages show his sacramental realism and his faith in the communion of saints.

## XX

The certainty of God's presence is so great that the most natural and down-to-earth things and circumstances reveal it in ways that we can handle and enjoy.

**58**  Heaven lies 'a foot and a half above the height of a man', in the words of an old Kerrywoman in the south-west of Ireland today, as homely and intimate as it was in the Middle Ages. The poem originated in the tenth or the eleventh century, and has continued in many various forms. Peig Sayers, *An Old Woman's Reflections*, translated from the Irish by Seamus Ennis (Oxford 1962); quotation from the introduction by W. R. Rodgers, p. xii.

**59**  See **57** above.

## XXI

Just as there is a time for feasting, so there is a time for fasting. Fullness comes from the acceptance that both of these have their part to play on the way to heaven.

**60**  Here is a simple rule for a solitary, versified. Shortened. Eighth-century. Kenneth Jackson, *Studies in Early Celtic Nature Poetry* (Cambridge 1935), pp. 105–6.

**61**  Gomer M. Roberts, *Y Per Ganiedydd* (Gwasg Aberystwyth), vol. i, p. 83. From a letter of Pantycelyn of 1744 (written in English).

## XXII

If we respond to Christ's call to follow him we cannot evade the cost of discipleship. Most of us will not be called to red martyrdom, but we may be asked to suffer in quieter but not less demanding ways.

**62** Whitley Stokes and John Strachan, *Thesaurus Palaeo-hibernicus*, vol. ii (Dublin 1903), pp. 224–7.
**63** Waldo Williams, *Dail Pren* (Gwasg Aberystwyth 1956), pp. 90–91. Verses from Waldo Williams's poem in praise of the Catholic martyrs of the Reformation period. Trans. H. A. Hodges.

# XXIII

'Joy and grief are woven fine.' Mary, mother of Christ, mother of us all, can help us because she knows them both equally.

**64** *Carmina Gadelica*, vol. iii, pp. 320–21. Here given in the translation by G. R. D. McClean, *Poems of the Western Highlanders* (SPCK 1961), p. 77.
**65** Waldo Williams, op. cit., p. 43. The poet writes about his own mother, the wife of a primary school teacher in the south-west of Wales.

# XXIV

The constant awareness that the Three in One guard and enrich us is frequently reflected in prayers and blessings.

**66** *Carmina Gadelica*, vol. iii, p. 63.
**67** M. Wynn Thomas, *Morgan Llwyd* (University of Wales Press 1984), p. 33. Morgan Llwyd (1619–59), visionary of the Commonwealth period; contacts with the first Quakers.

# XXV

The images of water and of oil, flowing, pouring, running, all speak to us of the cleansing and healing properties of the Spirit who brings life and fruitfulness.

**68** *Carmina Gadelica*, vol. iii, p. 205.
**69** T. M. Charles-Edwards, *Two Medieval Welsh Poems* (Gomer Press 1971). Lines from a poem about St Winifred's well at Holywell, by Tudor Aled (1480–1526).

## XXVI

St Columba by his journey linked Ireland and Scotland. Iona becomes a visible sign of that invisible network which links different places, different peoples, angels and men in the communion of saints.

**70** Attributed to St Columba. Early twelfth-century. Kenneth Jackson, *Studies in Early Celtic Poetry*, pp. 9–10. Shortened.
**71** D. M. and E. M. Lloyd, op. cit., pp. 269–70. The original of Gwenallt translated by D. M. Lloyd. Shortened.

## XXVII

On the threshold of death the urgency of repentance becomes a reality, but dying loses its terror in face of the promise of God's forgiving love.

**72** From Ann MacDonald, widow, from Lochaber. *Carmina Gadelica*, vol. iii, pp. 389–91.
**73** Joseph P. Clancy, *The Earliest Welsh Poetry*, pp. 149–50. Poems of repentance at the end of life were composed by many medieval poets. This one is by Cynddelw Brydydd Mawr.

## XXVIII

We do not find Christ at the end of the journey unless he accompanies us along the way.

**74** Kuno Meyer, op. cit., p. 100.
**75** *Llyfr Emynau a Thonau*, 589 or 2 and 3; 678, v. 4. Selected verses from Pantycelyn. Trans. H. A. Hodges.

## XXIX

Angels and archangels and all the company of heaven surround us.

**76** Robin Flower, *The Irish Tradition* (Oxford 1947), p. 48.
**77** *Llyfr Emynau a Thonau*, 331. The first verse is by Robert Jones, Caergybi (1731–1806); verses 2 and 3 anonymous. Trans. H.A.H.

## XXX

As the threshold of each day brings the certainty of new light, so we can hold to the promise of the final and eternal light which awaits us at the end of our journeying.

**78** Invocations. *Carmina Gadelica*, vol. i, p. 33.
**79** *Llyfr Emynau a Thonau*, 513. William Williams, Pantycelyn. Trans. H.A.H.

# Acknowledgements

Thanks are due to the Scottish Academic Press, Edinburgh, for kind permission to quote from vols. i and iii of *Carmina Gadelica, Hymns and Incantations, with Illustrative Notes of Words, Rites and Customs Dying and Obsolete:* Orally collected in the Highlands and Islands of Scotland by Alexander Carmichael, vol. i edited by Mrs. E. C. Watson, vol. iii by Professor James Carmichael Watson.

The illustrations are taken from vol. i of *Carmina Gadelica*, by permission.

The editors are also grateful to the following for permission to use copyright material. The numbers (printed in bold type) refer to the pages in this collection on which the quotations occur. Full bibliographical details are given in the Notes on pp. **82-93**; The Banner of Truth Trust **35**, **47**; Ruth Bidgood **39**; Dr. Euros Bowen **55**; Cambridge University Press **26**, **60**, **70**; Dr. T. M. Charles-Edwards **69**; Dr. Joseph P. Clancy **21**, **45**, **73**; Constable Publishers **32**, **50**, **74**; Curtis Brown Ltd **31**; Gomer Press **29**, **51**, **57**, **59**, **61**, **63**, **65**; Macmillan, London and Basingstoke **27**; Mary M. Martin **32**; Oxford University Press **30**, **36**, **46**, **58**, **76**; A. D. Peters & Co Ltd **28**, **48**, **54**; Poetry Wales Press **33**; Routledge & Kegan Paul Ltd **42**, **52**; SPCK **22**, **40**, **64**; University of Wales Press **23**, **37**, **49**, **67**; Veritas Publications **34**.

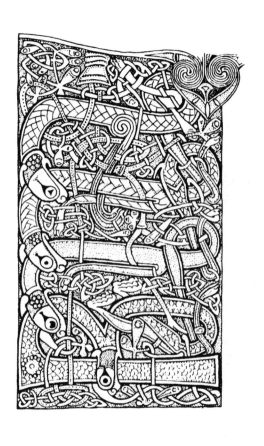